# ANTELOPES

## AFRICAN ANIMAL DISCOVERY LIBRARY

Lynn M. Stone

Rourke Corporation, Inc.
Vero Beach, Florida 32964

PHOTO CREDITS

All photos by the Author

**LIBRARY OF CONGRESS**
**Library of Congress Cataloging-in-Publication Data**
Stone, Lynn M.
    Antelopes / by Lynn M. Stone.

    p. cm. — (African animal discovery library)
    Summary: An introduction to the physical characteristics,
habits, and natural environment of the various species of African
antelope.
    ISBN 0-86593-053-8
    1. Antelopes—Juvenile literature. [1. Antelopes.] I. Title.
II. Series: Stone, Lynn M. African animal discovery library.
QL737.U53S743   1990
599.73'58—dc20                        89-48435
                                         CIP
Printed in the USA                       AC

*Leopard with topi kill*

# TABLE OF CONTENTS

# ANTELOPES

The African antelopes belong to a large group of mammals with horns. There are more than 70 **species,** or kinds, of African antelopes.

Antelope vary in size from the rabbit-sized dik-dik to the cow-sized giant eland. Dik-diks weigh as little as four pounds. Eland weigh up to 1900 pounds!

Antelopes chew a **cud,** like cows and several other grass-eating animals. The cud is food which is pumped from the stomach back into the mouth for more chewing.

Many antelopes have strange names. The blesbok, duiker, and wildebeeste were named by Dutch settlers in Africa. French settlers named the oryx and gazelle. Kongoni and impala are antelope names taken from the Swahili language of Africa.

*Grant's gazelle*

## THE ANTELOPES' COUSINS

Antelopes are related to buffalo, sheep, goats, cattle, and bison. These animals are what scientists call bovines.

Bovines are plant eaters, chew a cud, and have two horns. The largest bovines are wild buffalo and cattle. Antelope are slimmer and more graceful than buffalo or cattle.

Wild bovines are found in most parts of the world. In North American, for example, there are wild sheep, mountain goats, and the American bison.

The pronghorn of western North America looks much like an African antelope. Many scientists, however, do not consider the pronghorn to be a close relative of African antelopes.

*American pronghorn*

## HOW THEY LOOK

Most antelopes have slender legs and bodies, like deer. You could easily mistake some antelopes for deer, but not the wildebeeste, or gnu (pronounced "new").

A wildebeeste antelope looks like it was made from spare parts of other animals. It appears to have the tail of a horse, the mane of a lion, and the horns of a buffalo.

Antelopes are gray, white, brown, black, or a mixture of those colors.

Antelopes grow a pair of horns which are never shed. They point upwards or backwards. Some species have horns which twist or curve.

9

*Impala*

## WHERE THEY LIVE

Most of the world's antelopes live on the continent of Africa. A few others live in Asia.

African antelopes live in many different kinds of places. Each type of place, such as grassland, is called a **habitat.**

Much of Africa is grassland with scattered patches of trees. This habitat is called **savanna.** Many of the antelopes live on the savannas. Some of the most commonly seen are the wildebeeste, impala, gazelle, hartebeeste, and topi.

*Hartebeeste*

Wildebeeste on
African savanna

## HOW THEY LIVE

Antelopes spend most of their time feeding, resting, and chewing their cuds.

Antelopes usually travel together in groups called **herds.** The herds move slowly along as the antelopes feed on grass and other plants.

Some herds **migrate** each year. When animals migrate, they travel from one place to another as seasons change. Many of the one and one-half million wildebeeste in East Africa spend the rainy season on the savannas. When the rains ends, they move on to look for better pastures.

*Lion with wildebeeste*

# THE ANTELOPES' BABIES

The babies of large antelopes, such as eland, are called calves. The young of smaller antelopes, like reedbuck, are known as fawns.

Most species of antelopes have one baby per year. Antelopes almost never have twins.

Baby antelopes either follow their mothers shortly after birth or they hide. Wildebeeste calves are followers. They can run just seven minutes after birth!

Eland calves are hidden in grass or thickets for two weeks. Reedbuck fawns stay hidden for up to four months.

If they escape their enemies and disease, some species of antelopes live for 20 years.

*Wildbeeste cow
and calf*

## PREDATOR AND PREY

All antelopes eat plants, but they do not all eat the same kinds of plants.

Gerenuk, for example are **browsers.** They use their mouths to snip leaves from trees. They can stand on their hind legs to reach branches.

Wildebeeste are **grazers.** They eat grass.

Antelopes are important food, or **prey,** for Africa's hunting animals, called **predators.** Antelopes which are healthy and full-grown can usually outrun predators, but sometimes lions, jackals, hyenas, wild dogs, leopards, lions, and cheetahs catch them by surprise.

Predators usually seek young, old, or sick antelopes for their prey.

*Cheetahs with antelope kill*

## ANTELOPES AND PEOPLE

Antelopes have always been important to people in Africa. Antelopes have been used for their meat and skins. (Antelope skin, or hide, is made into leather.)

African farmers have killed thousands of antelopes. Farmers want to save the wild grasses for their cattle. The bluebuck antelope of South Africa is **extinct**—gone forever—because of too much shooting.

Hunting, the loss of antelope habitat for farms, and the spread of diseases from farm animals have hurt antelopes in Africa.

*Eland in*
*Nairobi National Park*

## THE ANTELOPES' FUTURE

Antelopes face many problems. The greatest problem is the loss of even more habitat, the antelopes' living places.

Africa's human population is growing rapidly. As more wild land is changed into farm and city, antelopes will have fewer places to live.

During dry periods, antelopes used to leave their homes and travel to wetter places with green plants. Many antelopes can no longer leave the dry places because farms block their path.

Thousands of African antelopes are protected in areas called reserves. In the future, reserves may become the only homes for wild antelopes.

# Glossary

**browser** (BROW zer)—an animal which feeds on leaves and twigs

**cud** (KUHD)—food which is chewed a second time after having already been chewed and swallowed once

**extinct** (ex TINKT)—the point at which an animal species no longer exists, such as the bluebuck

**grazer** (GRAY zer)—an animal which feeds on grass or other low plants of the field

**habitat** (HAB a tat)—the kind of place an animal lives in, such as grassland

**herd** (HERD)—a group of large, hoofed animals, such as antelopes

**migrate** (MY grate)—to make a regular journey from one certain place to another as a change of season takes place

**predator** (PRED a tor)—an animal that kills another animal for food

**prey** (PREY)—an animal that is hunted by another animal for food

**savanna** (sa VAN nuh)—broad, grassy areas with few trees

**species** (SPEE sheez)—within a group of closely related animals, one certain kind

# INDEX